CLASSIC AMERICAN FARM GAS ENGINES

Photography by Dave Arnold

Text by C. H. Wendel

Motorbooks International
Publishers & Wholesalers Inc
Osceola, Wisconsin 54020, USA ®

To Molly Jean, my first born. Thanks for your love of life and happy nature.

First published in 1988 by Motorbooks International Publishers & Wholesalers Inc, P O Box 2, 729 Prospect Avenue, Osceola, WI 54020 USA

Printed and bound in Hong Kong

Library of Congress
Cataloging-in-Publication Data
Arnold, Dave.
   Classic American farm gas engines.

   1. Farm engines--Pictorial works.
I. Wendel, C. H. (Charles H.)
II. Title.
TJ712.A76 1988   631.3'7   88-12871
ISBN 0-87938-313-5

On the front cover: *Twin City tractors from Minneapolis Steel & Machinery Company represented another important part of the farm equipment industry. In 1929 Minneapolis-Moline Corporation was formed when Minneapolis Steel merged with Moline Plow Company and Minneapolis Threshing Machine Company.*

On the frontispiece: *Oliver Farm Equipment Company was formed in 1929 and resulted from a merger of several companies. Among them was Oliver Chilled Plow Company and Hart-Parr Company. For a short time after the merger the tractors carried the Oliver-Hart-Parr designation.*

On the title page: *Today's large steam engine shows ostensibly began as a group of farmers getting together to literally relive the good old days. Their activities might have been confined to a threshing bee, or as is the case here, cutting silage the old-fashioned way.*

On this page: *A Novo engine built in the typical vertical design. And obviously restored to within an inch of its life.*

On the back cover: *McCormick-Deering engines were built exclusively in a throttling governor design: standard four-cycle engines which fired on every power stroke. Hit-and-miss engines, on the other hand, fired only when the governor sensed the need. Otherwise the governor mechanism held the exhaust valve open, allowing the engine to coast in the interim.*

Contents

Introduction

One of the best-kept secrets of our time is the phenomenal development of the gas engine. It has come from a crude, heavy, noisy and largely undependable machine of a century ago to the highly tuned engine of today, complete with electronic ignition, fuel injection and complete computerized control of engine functions. Whether it seems possible or not, today's sophisticated designs are direct descendants of those huge engines that weighed something on the order of 300 pounds per delivered horsepower!

Gas—meaning natural gas or some other form of explosive gas—was first used as an engine fuel. Gasoline and other liquid fuels were not sufficiently developed in the 1870s, and in fact, after liquid fuels became available, several decades passed before efficient carburetor designs appeared. A cursory glance at just one month of the *Patent Office Gazette* in the early 1900s shows that literally dozens of carburetor patents were issued, month after month and year after year, all in an effort to render the most efficient conversion of liquid fuels into a gaseous form suitable for operating an engine. Although it is easy to stand on a distant hill and suggest what our progenitors *might have done,* our disparagement is

tempered somewhat when it is considered that decades hence, we might well be subject to the same criticisms.

Carburetion is but one area that required, and continues to require, constant research. Ignition had its problems too. The Otto engine of 1876—the first four-cycle engine in the world—used a mechanically complicated open flame system of ignition. Etienne Lenoir's non-compressing engine of an earlier time used electric ignition, but Nicolaus August Otto considered this too unreliable for commercial use. Ignition systems then used the so-called hot-tube system up to about 1900, and finally, electric ignition was developed to the point that it was reliable and dependable.

The mechanically complicated but electrically simple make-and-break

These tractors in tandem typify the American farmer of the 1930s as he plowed the fields for a new crop. Particularly in the Midwest, moldboard plowing was one of the major duties for the tractor. The task often required every ounce of available power, especially when working in heavy soils.

ignition system depended on an inductance coil in series with the battery and a set of points within the engine cylinder. By mechanically opening these points very quickly, a big orange spark was created and ignition followed. Spark plug or high-tension ignition systems were electrically complicated but mechanically simple as well. These systems were in wide use by 1915, at least in stationary engines.

Internal combustion engines generally used a fairly long stroke, compared to the engine bore. As an example, an 8 horsepower engine might have been designed with a 6x10 inch bore and stroke, along with a top speed of perhaps 225 revolutions per minute. The low speed was imperative to prevent self-destruction of the huge flywheels, and was often the maximum speed at which the automatic, atmospherically operated intake valve and much of the mechanism could function efficiently.

Another interesting aspect of the early engines is the various governor systems used. Aside from specific types, two major forms of governing were in vogue: hit-and-miss and volume.

The earliest to be used was the hit-and-miss design. In most cases, this system depended on the governor actuating a finger which would engage a catch block on the exhaust valve pushrod, holding it open when the engine had attained its proper speed. This allowed the engine to coast until the speed dropped sufficiently for the governor finger to retract, permitting the exhaust valve to close, and followed by the normal cycle of events. In the jargon of the enthusiast, the hit-and-miss engine operated by firing a shot, and then running for several revolutions before it unhooked and did the same thing all over again. This type of

governor system was the most commonly used on farm-type engines.

Volume governing systems depended on the governor to operate a butterfly in the carburetor throat. With this system the air-fuel mixture remained at a constant value but the volume or amount of mixture entering the cylinder was under the control of the governor. This system was developed in the 1890s and was virtually identical to the governor found on anything from a small air-cooled engine to a big tractor motor.

Stationary and portable gas engines were used for virtually any task on the farmstead that could be accomplished with motive power. Few farms of the early 1900s had electricity, and even if it was available, rare indeed was the use of electric motor power on the farm. Gas engines, however, could be readily adapted for anything from running the washing machine to sawing wood or shelling corn. Oftentimes a single engine on a farm was used for a multitude of duties.

Looking past the big flywheels and the cast iron, these engines did in fact operate much like today's small air-cooled designs. The heavily proportioned parts and a very low operating speed made it almost impossible to wear out one of these engines, given reasonable care.

The earliest gas tractors simply adapted large stationary gas engines to a chassis. In fact, the early International Harvester tractors used the company's

A display of vintage tractors brings to mind the great diversity of design evident in American farm tractors. Of the tractors in the foreground, about the only common features are a pair of front wheels beneath a gigantic cast-iron radiator!

own engines on a Morton chassis to enter the tractor business. Others like Hart-Parr and Rumely built engines specifically for their tractors, but these were of extremely heavy construction and used a relatively low operating speed. Like the stationary engines from which they descended, the early tractor engines featured almost every conceivable configuration of cylinder position: vertical, horizontal and somewhere in between.

Cooling systems saw no limits—every manufacturer had its own ideas about the ideal system. The fact is that most cooling systems worked reasonably well, especially when it is considered that the best water available was often contaminated with dirt and other foreign material which eventually plugged the cooling passages.

Tractor lubrication was a perpetual problem—the huge cast-iron gear teeth could be reduced to razor sharpness and early failure under certain conditions. Two schools of thought prevailed. One said that no lubrication was better than applying grease to the gears, which would subsequently attract dust and grit like a magnet. Others decided that even gritty grease was better than none at all. Engine lubrication assumed every form, from simple drip oilers to mechanical lubricators to splash systems, or combinations thereof.

The cross-mounted tractor engine was intended to obviate the need for

This visitor to a vintage engine show is probably recalling the bittersweet past as he watches this International Harvester engine strut its stuff. In many respects, "old engine" shows are probably as much a celebration of our agrarian past as they are a tribute to those sturdy individuals who toil for weeks on end to bring an old engine back to life.

extensive bevel gearing systems from engine to drivetrain. With the cross-mounted engine, all that was necessary was a train of simple spur gears—the ultimate in simplicity. The Wallis tractor of J. I. Case Plow Works was the first model to change this notion. Their tractor had all the gears enclosed and operating in oil, out of the dirt and grit. With the development of tapered roller bearings came the Fordson tractor with its worm gear final drive system. Under heavy loads it became very hot due to the excessive friction; some farmers said the transmission case "got hot enough to fry eggs."

Despite the many problems of early tractors, design improvements continued at a steady pace. In fact, the development of the farm tractor represents a classic case of steady evolutionary development; each new idea became the building block for yet another improvement. Although some designs of this early period may now come under ridicule, it must always be remembered that even the poor ideas were, for the most part, a lot better than anything in the past.

Today, a substantial number of shows and exhibitions are held annually to celebrate the development of vintage engines, tractors and farm equipment. For those who actually operated these machines it is a time of nostalgia, a time when vivid memories of pleasant and unpleasant times can be recalled and probably retold. For those of us who have come later, these fine mechanical artifacts stand as a wonderful tribute to those sturdy individuals who were determined to make life better for themselves, and for us!

Stationary engines

Nicholaus August Otto's 1876 patent brought the four-cycle engine into a practical reality. By the following year Otto engines were for sale in the United States. Steady improvement followed, but the Otto design remained fairly constant, even with this 1895 model. The engine shown here was rated at 10.9 horsepower. Otto tested each engine individually at the factory and recorded its output on the nameplate.

Old-time gasoline engines are now highly sought after collector items. Thousands of enthusiasts gather annually at many different exhibitions all over the United States. At a typical display such as this, one will see many different sizes and styles—common and uncommon.

Although Fairbanks-Morse engines were not shipped from the factory with any striping to adorn the dark green enamel, a homebrew combination of designs brightens this particular example. Very early engines were often highly adorned with striping and lettering. Powerful competition required cost-cutting, and this meant an end to fancy decorations.

A typical exhibit at a vintage engine show includes many different makes and models, with most engines in operation, but not belted to a load. This little engine of about 1½ horsepower would typically have been used to pump water, operate a small feed grinder or accomplish other duties about the farmstead.

17

This trio of McCormick-Deering engines represent the 1½, 3 and 6 horsepower sizes. A big 10 horsepower model was also built. Shown here in their unrestored state, these engines have probably seen countless hours of duty, and are still restorable to like-new condition.

Among other machines, John Deere
Tractor Company built a most
impressive series of engines in 1½, 3
and 6 horsepower models. This fully
restored set is among the most
popular line of engines sought after
by today's collectors.

21

Previous page
During the 1930s, International
Harvester Company introduced the
lightweight, high-speed engines
shown here. Two sizes were built,
1½ to 2½ horsepower, and 3 to 5
horsepower. The odd horsepower
rating resulted from the fact that by
adjusting the engine throttle, engine
speed and the resultant horsepower
output were changed.

Engine designs ran the entire gamut
from the simple to the sublime. The
Stickney engine was of a peculiar
design, totally different than any
other engine on the market. Despite
its unique appearance the Stickney
enjoyed considerable popularity for
a few years. This 5 horsepower
model dates back to about 1914.

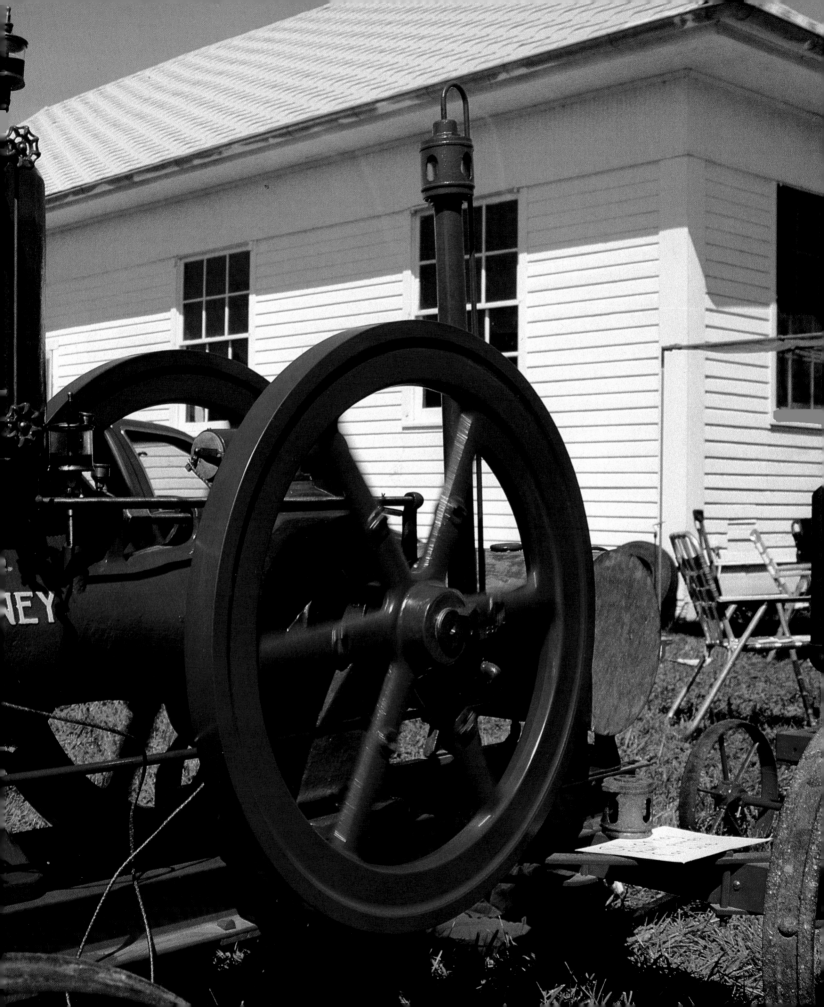

Previous page
So-called headless engines were fairly popular with farmers. The 1½ horsepower Fairbanks-Morse model in the foreground is a typical example. While slightly more difficult to cast and machine, the headless design eliminated problems with head gaskets.

The typical farm engine was built in a horizontal design, although companies like Novo of Lansing, Michigan, made this vertical model very popular. The company name was derived from the Latin novus, meaning "new."

The ball-shaped dome of this Monitor engine is actually the jacket for the cooling water. It could have been almost any shape, but when Baker Manufacturing Company of Evansville, Wisconsin, adapted this pleasing design they also made the Monitor name synonymous with a unique and very popular engine.

Virtually every possible head configuration was used in some vintage engine. As shown above, the exhaust valve is closed allowing the intake valve to open. To the right, the exhaust is held open by the governor, allowing the engine to free-wheel. Only the exhaust valve of this engine was mechanically operated. The automatic intake valve depended entirely on its operation from the intake stroke of the piston. The design was very simple but had definite limitations.

Previous page
Numerous museums have amassed
an impressive array of vintage
engines during the past couple
decades. Curiously, few museum
visitors realize that these huge cast-
iron behemoths of yesteryear are
direct ancestors—blood relatives—
to today's lightweight, high-speed
engines. By contrast, none of the
engines illustrated here could
operate above perhaps 500
revolutions per minute!

Some companies built special
pumping engines, using designs
intended specifically for this duty.
Most were adaptable to almost any
existing pump standard, and like this
Fuller & Johnson model, they were
securely clamped to the pump
standard. The pump arms, not
shown in this photograph, were then
connected to the pump rod, and
presto! it was no longer necessary to
pump water by hand.

Pumping water by hand might have
been a good muscle builder, but it
fell among the drudgery and tedium
of farm life without the benefit of
mechanical power. Working the
handle of this old-time power pump
of the early 1900s was not an
enjoyable task.

Hydraulic rams were another method of pumping water. These rather simple devices depended on kinetic energy to raise water pressure at the sacrifice of volume, and in so doing, a certain amount of water was lost. These losses were negligible, however, when compared to the great advantages secured.

36

A few power pumps of an earlier time actually used elliptical gearing to provide a rather fast downward stroke of the pump plunger, but a slower upward stroke. This raised the pumping capacity but permitted a rather small engine to be used. American ingenuity constantly came through, even on something as simple as a pump jack.

Another task desperately needing gas engine power was that of felling and bucking trees. Antedating the chain saw, this Witte log saw of the 1920s is ready for action. The special linkage system driving the saw was usually designed to closely imitate the action of a two-man hand saw.

38

Now a rarity, this old-time shingle mill is in operation at a vintage engine and machinery show. Cedar blocks are preferred. The shingle mill uses a unique mechanism which allows it to grip the block during the sawing process, alternating its position so that the shape is maintained. Beyond providing an interesting demonstration, the shingle saw is also giving some exercise to a vintage tractor.

Maytag Company gained immense fame with their power washing machine, and also provided a small engine tailor-made to operate it. Maytag washers were highly instrumental in eliminating the drudgery of hand-washing, with the company continuing to build on its early success in this field.

Fancy decals were often used on early engines. This Root & Vandervoort engine of the 1914-18 period is adorned with a bright, multicolored logo. These small engines were used for a multitude of farm jobs from shelling corn and pumping water to grinding sausage.

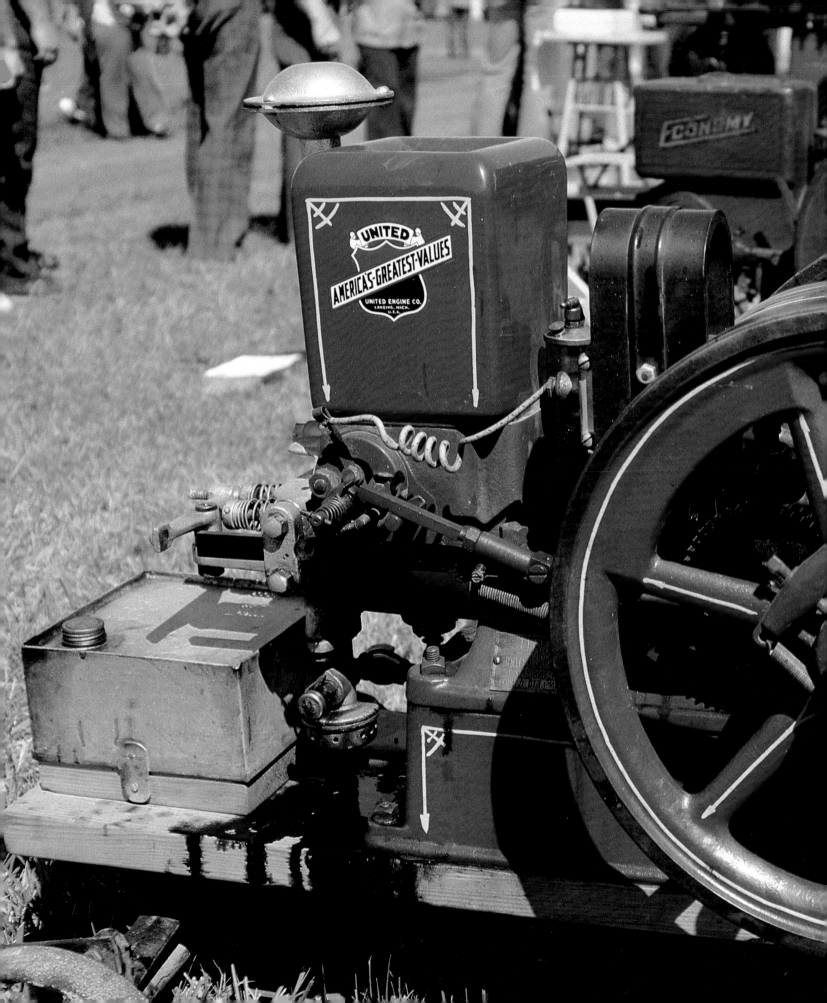

United engines were very popular and used a bright red finish, together with a beautiful decal and striping. This engine was actually built at Waterloo, Iowa, by Associated Manufacturers, even though United operated from Lansing, Michigan. In fact, many parts were interchangeable between United and Associated engines.

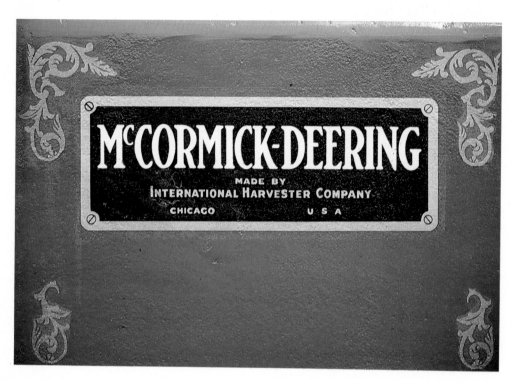

The McCormick-Deering trademark adorned thousands of engines. Built with a first-class design and sold by a first-rate dealer network, these engines further magnified the success of International Harvester Company.

Bright colors characterized some engines, as seen on this Galloway of about 1914. William Galloway was a master salesman and an undisputed expert in the mailorder business. Galloway's slogan as "The House That Divides the Melon with its Customers" won a great many steady customers for Galloway products.

Many engine builders embellished their engines with expensive cast-brass nameplates. One example is this Fairbanks-Morse builder's plate that includes patents from 1892 to 1901, and as the plate says, "Other Patents Pending." Indeed there were; Fairbanks-Morse accumulated engine patents by the hundreds.

48

AIRBANKS
MORSE
& COMPANY
PATENTED
2-N° 472106 | MAY·18·1897·N° 582620
2-N° 477295 | JUL·6·1897·N° 585652
5-N° 542043 | AUG·8·1899·N° 630624
OCT·15·1901·N° 684662
HER PATENTS PENDING

Many companies offered engines under their own trademark, even though they did not actually manufacture the engines they sold. A typical example is the Rock Island engine shown here. Sold by the famous plow company of the same name, this engine was actually manufactured by Alamo Manufacturing Company of Hillsdale, Michigan.

51

Light tractors

A J. I. Case portable steam engine was the first widely accepted step in bringing any sort of prime mover to rural areas. An engine like this was able to power a small sawmill or thresher, and while it required four horses to move it from place to place, this was much easier than doing everything by hand. The steam engine was reliable too, compared to waiting for the wind to blow so the windmill could be used, or compared to postponing use of a water wheel when the creek was too low.

A simple steam engine like this one merely used steam on both sides of the piston to deliver power to a flywheel. The exhaust steam was piped to a vertical nozzle in the smokestack to create an induced draft over the fire. Tandem compound engines placed two separate cylinders and pistons on the same piston rod. Steam was expanded first in the smaller, high-pressure cylinder; then traveled to the larger, low-pressure cylinder. Cross-compound engines followed the same principles but mounted the high- and low-pressure cylinders on separate engine cranks. Increased fuel economy was the objective of compounding, but the results were elusive, given the relatively low boiler pressures used at the time.

54

Previous page

Huber Manufacturing Company at Marion, Ohio, was one of the early steam engine and thresher builders. Their cross-mounted tractor design of the 1920s enjoyed at least some popularity, and although it did not sell as well as the Titan of International Harvester, it was nevertheless of excellent design.

The Wallis tractor of J. I. Case Plow Works heralded the unit-frame design, and although many claimed that Fordson was the first unit-frame tractor, the Wallis "boiler-plate" frame preceded it by several years. The rolled steel plate served as the tractor frame and also doubled as the engine crankcase.

Previous page
Fred Bruns of Hecla, South Dakota,
is the proud pilot of this grand old
OilPull tractor built by Advance-
Rumely Thresher Company of
LaPorte, Indiana. The OilPull owed
its name and its success to its unique
capability of burning virtually any
low-grade fuel at any load, and
doing it successfully!

Although a few companies had
adapted an in-line engine mounting
by the 1920s, many, like this J. I.
Case model, continued with a cross-
mounted engine. Intended to
minimize problems from
troublesome bevel gearing to the
drivetrain, the cross-mount design
eventually fell out of favor.

Waterloo Boy tractors were immensely popular in the midwestern states, and were a major basis for today's John Deere tractor line. This resulted from Deere's 1918 purchase of Waterloo Gasoline Engine Company of Waterloo, Iowa.

Previous page
One of the most popular tractors in the midwestern states, and for that matter, almost everywhere else, was the Titan 10-20 of International Harvester Company. The Titan was the strongest adversary encountered by Henry Ford when he introduced his Fordson tractor. The Titan was built from 1915 to 1922.

The cross-mounted engine design in many tractors, including this Rumely OilPull, did not leave sufficient clearance between the right front wheel and a drive belt, so a special shifting device was provided that permitted the operator to easily shift the front axle several inches out of the way. This axle was already in position for belt work, but had to be shifted back for plowing or other field work.

Cross-mounted engines were an obvious design feature of early Minneapolis tractors. The builder was Minneapolis Threshing Machine Company; they later merged with Minneapolis Steel and Machinery and Moline Plow Company to form the gigantic Minneapolis-Moline Corporation.

Long retired from active service, this vintage model Twin City tractor has been restored to like-new condition and is now preserved as a reminder of our agricultural past. Thousands of similar tractors were cut up during the scrap iron drives of World War II.

Previous page
The Oliver Row-Crop 70 of 1935 presented a very attractive streamlined hood design that soon characterized much of American farm tractor design. Also evident was the Power on Tiptoe concept, a term used by Oliver to describe their open-faced skeleton wheels.

Prior to the introduction of rubber tires for tractors came a concerted effort for improved steel wheel designs. These included the Oliver "tiptoe" design shown here. Despite a certain amount of popularity, Oliver's Power on Tiptoe wheels were quickly replaced with rubber tires as soon as they became available.

74

John Deere offered a so-called skeleton wheel design for some of their row-crop tractors during the 1930s. When Allis-Chalmers announced the first rubber-tired tractor in 1931, reactions were initially negative, especially among competing tractor companies. Eventually, however, the power losses created from pushing these lugs into the soil and pulling them out again forced a new look and eventual acceptance of rubber tires.

75

TWIN CITY LUGS
FORMED & BUILT BY LARSON WELDING & MACHINE
Ray Shoberg • Norman Pross • Jim Briden
1985

Guardians of our public roads can add an entirely new dimension to the term irate when someone happens to drive those heavy steel lugs across a glass-smooth blacktop surface. To maintain the aesthetic appearance of the original design and still protect roadways from damage, these individuals have developed non-marring attachment lugs.

Virtually every tractor builder offered each of their models in a variety of configurations, each intended for specific crop conditions or local farming practices. This John Deere with its wide front axle represents one such derivative that never achieved celebrity status in terms of total production.

Previous page
This J. I. Case tractor of the 1930s sits in retirement, awaiting the masterful touch of an enthusiast who will patiently rebuild it to its former glory. In the process, the homebrew front tires and rims will be removed and replaced with original iron.

This fine-looking John Deere A tractor might well have been discovered in a farm grove, or worse yet, in a salvage yard about to endure the final indignity of a sledge hammer. As it is, however, this one has been completely restored—a job ultimately requiring several hundred hours, plus lots of tender loving care.

80

Previous page
Introduced in 1932 the Farmall F-12 of International Harvester was an immensely popular two-plow size. Originally built with steel wheels, it was later available on rubber tires. Farmers also drove thousands of steel-wheeled tractors to local blacksmith shops where new rims were welded in place and rubber tires installed.

A display of vintage tractors shows a tiny portion of a Rumely OilPull in the foreground. In the background, however, is an immensely attractive Silver King tractor. First introduced about 1936 the Silver King promenaded a design far ahead of its time.

Previous page
An attractive young lady graces an already attractive John Deere unstyled Model B tractor, while teaching a youngster the rudiments of tractor driving. Unstyled Deere tractors were built through 1939. The term refers to the total lack of hood metal around the radiator and steering post.

The bright red and gold colors of the Minneapolis-Moline tractors were an unmistakable sight on the American landscape. These tractors captured a substantial portion of the market into the 1950s, with their long-stroke, slow-speed engine being a major selling point.

Previous page

The Farmall tractor in the foreground is hitched to a McCormick-Deering combine operated from the tractor's power takeoff shaft. This 1920s development proved to be one of the most significant improvements in farm tractor design to that time.

Always a symbol of superiority, the eagle in cast iron adorned the radiator cap of Hart-Parr tractors. This Charles City, Iowa, company was America's first firm organized solely for the production of farm tractors.

A characteristic of many early farm tractors and implements came in the form of ornate trademark designs. The artwork alone was very expensive, and manufacturing these huge decals came as a substantial expense. But manufacturers were willing to pay it as a means of giving their machines immediate recognition by anyone, even those not necessarily familiar with power farming.

95

Whether burning distillate or kerosene, tractor engines were always started on gasoline. This required a small auxiliary tank, usually holding about a gallon of gasoline. Deere built theirs right into the rear of the main tank. The endbell served as a handy location for the John Deere trademark.

97

A line-up of light tractor seats at a show. Although the seats had a built-in suspension system and were air-cooled due to the holes drilled through the saddle, they were a chore to ride on throughout a day of hard work.

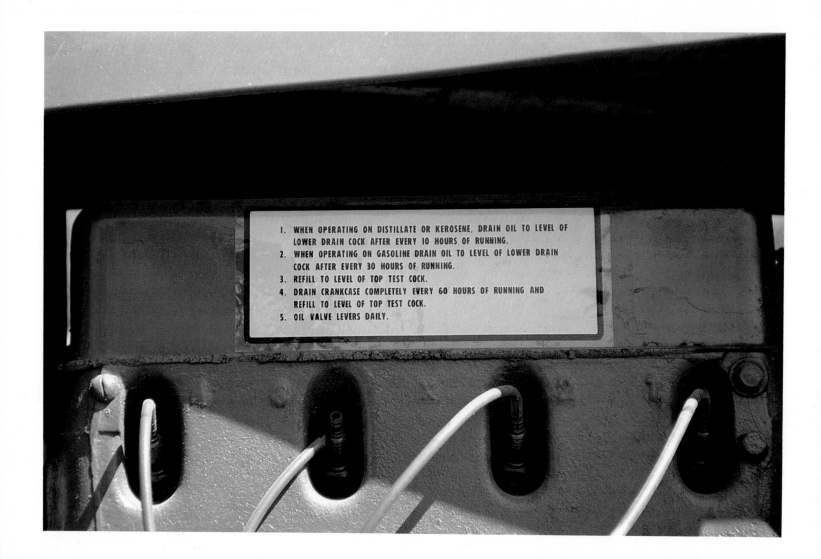

1. WHEN OPERATING ON DISTILLATE OR KEROSENE, DRAIN OIL TO LEVEL OF LOWER DRAIN COCK AFTER EVERY 10 HOURS OF RUNNING.
2. WHEN OPERATING ON GASOLINE DRAIN OIL TO LEVEL OF LOWER DRAIN COCK AFTER EVERY 30 HOURS OF RUNNING.
3. REFILL TO LEVEL OF TOP TEST COCK.
4. DRAIN CRANKCASE COMPLETELY EVERY 60 HOURS OF RUNNING AND REFILL TO LEVEL OF TOP TEST COCK.
5. OIL VALVE LEVERS DAILY.

Realizing that many farmers of the 1920s had no previous experience with tractors, most manufacturers used large-size decals that included most basics of engine maintenance. With the 1920s rage for burning low-grade fuels came the chronic problem of crankcase dilution. Avoiding it required frequent attention to the oil level, and often demanded draining diluted oil from the crankcase and adding new, fresh oil.

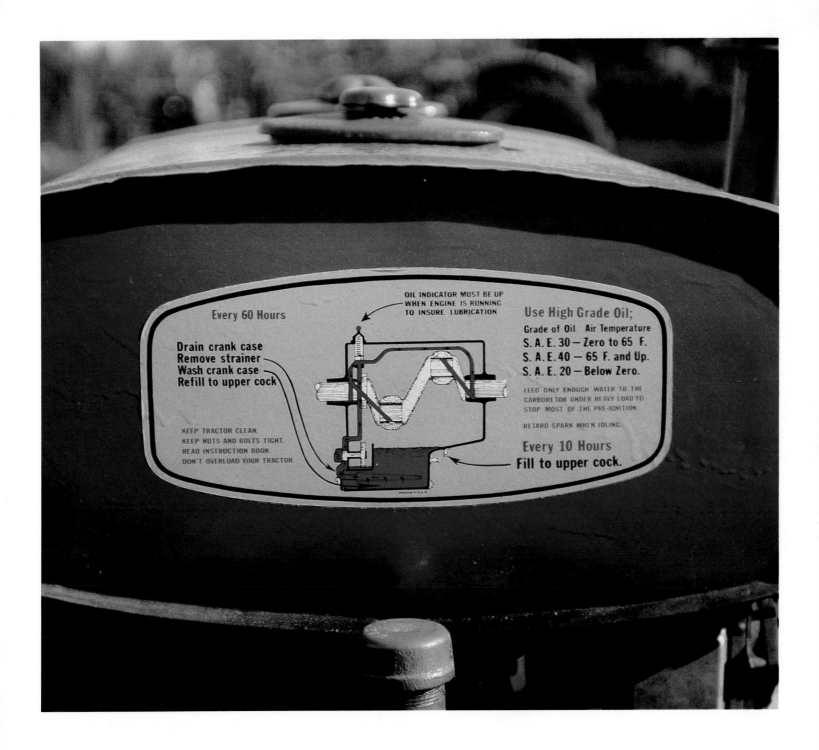

Every 60 Hours

Drain crank case
Remove strainer
Wash crank case
Refill to upper cock

OIL INDICATOR MUST BE UP
WHEN ENGINE IS RUNNING
TO INSURE LUBRICATION

Use High Grade Oil;

Grade of Oil   Air Temperature
S. A. E. 30 — Zero to 65 F.
S. A. E. 40 — 65 F. and Up.
S. A. E. 20 — Below Zero.

FEED ONLY ENOUGH WATER TO THE
CARBURETOR UNDER HEAVY LOAD TO
STOP MOST OF THE PRE-IGNITION.

RETARD SPARK WHEN IDLING.

KEEP TRACTOR CLEAN.
KEEP NUTS AND BOLTS TIGHT.
READ INSTRUCTION BOOK.
DON'T OVERLOAD YOUR TRACTOR.

Every 10 Hours
Fill to upper cock.

John Deere Tractor Company used this four-color decal to inform the operator of the required duties in servicing the tractor. The decal was situated on the rear of the fuel tank and within constant view of the operator. Its attractive design probably aided its purpose as a daily reminder of required lubrication checks.

ALWAYS CLOSE NEEDLE VALVES
BEFORE SWITCHING FROM ONE
FUEL TO ANOTHER • WHEN BOTH
VALVES ARE OPEN AT ONE TIME
THE FUELS WILL MIX • THIS
MAKES IT IMPOSSIBLE TO START

DISENGAGE CLU
BEFORE SHIFT
CLUTCH

*The instruction decal on this
International Harvester tractor
cautions the operator not to mix the
gasoline and kerosene fuels by
having both tank valves open at
once. Kerosene or distillate was
often chosen for heavy work, but
gasoline was always used for
starting the engine. The small tank
in the foreground is the auxiliary
tank for starting fuel; behind it is the
big main tank of probably 30 gallons
capacity.*

Tractor builders were often concerned that farmers remember specific instructions, with this Hart-Parr carrying the message "Watch Your Valve Clearance" on the valve cover. The message was an important one—too little or too much clearance was sure to cause trouble. In time, farmers familiarized themselves with tractor engines to the point that messages cast in iron were no longer necessary.

Cranking a balky or flooded engine by hand can be a horrendous task—pulling an 8 inch piston over dead center takes a long handle and lots of muscle! A John Deere comes to the rescue of this stubborn OilPull by means of a drive belt between the two. Clouds of white smoke from the OilPull indicate that success might be imminent, or is it? The small tank on the front of the Rumely radiator is simply an expansion tank for the engine coolant.

In the late 1940s the Willys Jeep gained wide attention as an all-around farm vehicle. Many different attachments were available, including this 2 bottom plow, connected to the Jeep in the background and ready for work. Despite an early flush of excitement, farmers turned to larger tractors, so the Jeep saw only a brief career as a willing farm servant.

Heavy tractors

A big 110 horsepower Case steamer prepares for a plowing demonstration. This huge engine used a cylinder having a 12 inch bore and stroke. Operating at perhaps 150 pounds per square inch or more, it could handle a huge 14 bottom plow without difficulty. Two men were required: an engineer to sit in the upper part of the cab and actually operate the engine, plus a fireman who worked on the lower platform.

Previous page
Like the farm tractors which followed, steam traction engines assumed every conceivable shape and size, often depending on the whim of the inventor. Advertising catalogs of the 1890s presented the various designs in glowing terms, often using terminology that even today requires a trip to the dictionary.

A huge, flat belt connects this steam traction engine with a sawmill. Almost forgotten are those sturdy individuals who developed canvas and rubber belting as an alternative to leather belts. The leather type possessed superior gripping abilities around a pulley but could be completely destroyed by rain. This, in addition to its cost, led to the development of canvas and rubber belting as a viable alternative.

A front view of the big 110 horsepower Case steam traction illustrates its awesome dimensions. These engines were used extensively with huge plows to turn over the boundless prairies of the United States and Canada. Although a substantial number were built, very few still exist.

This fully restored 10-20 International Titan tractor now spends most of its time "showing off" at vintage engine and tractor shows. The big red clutch pulley was a standard feature. It had the disadvantage of requiring the operator to start and stop the belted load by pulling or pushing on the large handwheel to the extreme left of this illustration.

Aultman-Taylor 30-60 tractors with their 8 foot drive wheels are always an impressive sight. Despite the reasonable success of this huge tractor, it had the distinct disadvantage of traveling only 2 miles per hour. During a busy threshing run, the long time required in moving from one farm to another at this speed occasionally gained it the nickname of Mud Turtle.

Large acreages on the Plains and in the western states often saw large crawler tractors like this Caterpillar model. The immense size of these tractors permitted one person to cover large areas in a relatively short time. The low center of gravity made the crawler ideal for hilly terrain—much more safe than a wheel tractor.

The steam engine is nearing a century in age, and despite its 12 tons in a tight parade route, this senior engineer feels just as comfortable with all this iron as a youngster with a trail bike. Achieving the status of steam engineer carried a special bit of prestige in its day, and now combines to form a poignant mixture of prestige, nostalgia and unmistakable pride.

121

Standing on the platform of a steam traction engine with its myriad valves and levers is indeed an awesome experience for the neophyte. Seasoned engineers, however, know which valves to turn and which levers to pull at just the right times. Not knowing will result in lots of steam and no place to go, or somewhere to go without any steam. Achieving the proper proportions between the two, often marked the difference between a good engineer and a lamentable representation of same.

123

A study of early tractor builders may seem to lead to the conclusion that these pioneering efforts were predicated on building a bigger tractor than the competition. This huge Pioneer tractor of about 1910 had rear wheels standing 9 feet high!

Probably a throwback to steam engine days, many early tractors were equipped with an operator cab. Ironically, this so-called luxury was almost completely abandoned until the 1960s when it reappeared, and finally ended up in today's sound-protected and air-conditioned tractor cabs. The only air conditioning in this cab is whatever the prevailing wind might provide.

125

Operating a steam engine required immense quantities of fuel and water. Since the exhaust steam went up the smokestack, several of these large loads were required each day. Originally the water wagons were equipped with a huge hand-operated pump. Team, wagon and driver drove to a nearby creek or other water source where the water was pumped into the tank by hand.

127

DATE DUE		
JUN 2 6 1989		
AUG 7 1989		
OC 12 '89		
FEB. 02 1990		
MAR. 09 1990		
MAR. 23 1990		
5-9		
5-16		
MR 25 '91		
MY 6 '91		
JUN. 2 0 1991		
OCT 2 8 1991		
JAN 1 4 1992		
JUN. 23 1993		
NOV 1 1994		

DEMCO 38-297